☞ **W9-BOG-319**

940.54   De Angelis,
DEA   Therese.
          Pearl Harbor :
          deadly surprise
          attack
PERMA-BOUND   BAR: 11P02872

DATE DUE			

$23.35

CLARK MIDDLE/HIGH
SCHOOL
1921 DAVIS AVENUE
WHITING, IN 46394

Pearl Harbor

Other titles in the *American Disasters* series:

Pearl Harbor
Deadly Surprise Attack

Therese De Angelis

AMERICAN DISASTERS

Enslow Publishers, Inc.

40 Industrial Road   PO Box 38
Box 398   Aldershot
Berkeley Heights, NJ 07922 Hants GU12 6BP
USA   UK

http://www.enslow.com

This book is dedicated to Judy L. Hasday—an
enthusiastic researcher, a fine writer, and a devoted
friend and colleague. Thanks for your support and
encouragement, Jude.

Copyright © 2002 by Enslow Publishers, Inc.

All rights reserved.

No part of this book may be reproduced by any means
without the written permission of the publisher.

Library of Congress Cataloging-in-Publication Data

De Angelis, Therese.
    Pearl Harbor : deadly surprise attack / Therese De Angelis.
        p. cm. — (American disasters)
    Includes bibliographical references and index.
    Summary: Traces events leading up to and resulting from the December 7, 1941,
Japanese attack on American battleships at Pearl Harbor, which brought the
United States into World War II.
    ISBN 0-7660-1783-4
    1. Pearl Harbor (Hawaii), Attack on, 1941—Juvenile literature. [1.Pearl Harbor
(Hawaii), Attack on, 1941. 2. World War, 1939-1945—Causes. 3. Japan—Foreign
relations—United States. 4. United States—Foreign relations—Japan.]   I. Title.
II. Series.
    D767.92 .D4   2002
    940.54'26—dc21
                                    2001003474

Printed in the United States of America

10 9 8 7 6 5 4 3 2 1

To Our Readers:
We have done our best to make sure all Internet addresses in this book were active
and appropriate when we went to press. However, the author and the publisher have
no control over and assume no liability for the material available on those Internet
sites or on other Web sites they may link to. Any comments or suggestions can be sent
by e-mail to comments@enslow.com or to the address on the back cover.

Illustration Credits: AP/Wide World Photos, pp. 6, 8, 21, 24, 28, 30, 37, 39; Enslow
Publishers, Inc., p. 12; Franklin D. Roosevelt Library, p. 35; National Archives,
pp. 14, 16, 20, 26, 34; U.S. Army Museum of Hawaii, p. 18; U.S. Naval Historical
Center, p. 1; U.S.S. Arizona Memorial, National Park Service, pp. 10, 23, 32.

Cover Illustration: AP/Wide World Photos.

Contents

An aerial photo of Pearl Harbor, Oahu, Hawaii. Hickam airfield can be seen in the foreground.

CHAPTER 1

"This Is Not A Drill!"

December 6, 1941, was an ordinary Saturday for the military personnel stationed at Pearl Harbor. Many United States soldiers and sailors on shore leave headed to Honolulu to visit a bar or buy souvenirs. Others stayed on base and swam in the new pool at Ford Island. Some saw a movie at Hickam Airfield's post theater. At the new recreation center, dance bands from the Pacific Fleet's ships competed in a "Battle of the Bands" contest. (The battleship *Pennsylvania*'s band won.)[1]

Admiral Husband E. Kimmel and Lieutenant General Walter C. Short were the highest-ranking military men at Pearl Harbor. Kimmel commanded the entire Pacific Fleet. Short was commander of the Hawaiian Department, in charge of defending Hawaii against attack. Short had taken steps to protect the base against spies and enemy attacks. He ordered all planes lined up outside their hangars, wingtip to wingtip, where they could easily be guarded against sabotage.[2] Sabotage is any secret enemy attempt to hinder a nation's ability to protect or defend itself. It was thought that by keeping the planes close together it would be easier to keep track of them.

As the night went on, enlisted men returned to their quarters and the base became quiet. After dinner, Lieutenant General Short returned home with his wife to Fort Shafter. He planned to join Admiral Kimmel early the next morning for a golf game and wanted to get a sound night's sleep.

At 7:55 A.M. on Sunday, December 7, Petty Officer George Campbell carried a cup of coffee and a news-paper onto the deck of the U.S.S. *Medusa.* The repair ship was anchored west of Ford Island. Just then he heard a roar overhead and saw several planes flying from the north toward Pearl Harbor. Campbell thought it was a practice drill by American pilots. He soon realized he was wrong. "We took a good look at the planes and saw the red-sun emblem [of the flag of Japan] and knew it was the real thing," he remembered.[3]

Lieutenant General Walter Short was commander of the Hawaiian Department of the Navy's Pacific Fleet. He was in charge of defending Hawaii against attack.

On the deck of the *Nevada*, members of the ship's band stood in formation and prepared to play the colors (music played while raising the American flag) and the national anthem. As they waited, they saw swarms of planes coming in low over Ford Island, toward Battleship Row where their ship was moored. They heard explosions, which quickly grew louder. At exactly 8:00 A.M., as the band began playing the "Star-Spangled Banner," one of the planes zoomed over the *Arizona*, which was in front of the *Nevada*, and dropped a torpedo. The plane turned away, spraying machine-gun fire at the *Nevada* and shredding the American flag as it was being raised. Band members completed the national anthem, and then dove for cover.[4]

At the Ford Island command center, Lieutenant Commander Logan Ramsey heard a screaming sound and was shocked to see a dive-bomber heading toward a nearby plane ramp. Ramsey thought it was a U.S. pilot behaving recklessly. Seconds later, an explosion rocked a nearby hangar, producing smoke and sending debris flying.

Ramsey realized that the plane was Japanese and that Pearl Harbor was under attack. He ran to the radio room where operators transmitted messages to the rest of the base. At 7:58 A.M., he ordered the radiomen on duty to send this message: "AIR RAID, PEARL HARBOR. THIS IS NOT A DRILL!"[5]

Pearl Harbor suffered two pounding air attacks from Japanese military forces that morning. A second wave of fighters shrieked over the base less than an hour after the

Sailors at the Kaneohe Naval Air Station attempt to save a burning plane after the Japanese attack on Pearl Harbor on December 7, 1941.

first attack. When the assault ended, 2,403 Americans were dead and 1,178 were wounded. Eight U.S. battleships were sunk or badly damaged. One hundred eighty-eight U.S. planes were destroyed or damaged.[6] The planes that were lined up wingtip to wingtip were destroyed more quickly and easily because they were so close together.

News of the surprise attack spread quickly. Stunned Americans realized that the United States was going to war.

CHAPTER 2

"The Power, the Purpose, and the Plan"

The islands of Hawaii lie about 2,400 miles southwest of San Francisco, California. These islands were formed millions of years ago, from lava that bubbled up from underwater volcanoes in the Pacific Ocean. You can still see active volcanoes on the islands today. The islands are known for their rich plant and animal life, tropical climate, beautiful waterfalls, and coral reefs.

The largest island of Hawaii is Oahu, where the state capital of Honolulu is located. (Hawaii became a U.S. state in 1959.) More than 830,000 people—about 75 percent of the state's population—live on Oahu.[1] Among the most famous sites on this island is the Pearl Harbor Naval Air Station (NAS). This is one of the world's largest naval bases. It dates to 1887, when the United States signed an agreement with the Kingdom of Hawaii to use the harbor for refueling and repairing ships. Later, the United States purchased more land around the harbor. Dry docks and a submarine base were built.

When Pearl Harbor was attacked in 1941, most of Europe was already fighting World War II. The war had broken out in 1939, after Germany invaded Poland. Great Britain and France had agreed to defend Poland, and so they declared war on Germany. In 1940 Germany conquered many European countries including France, Denmark, and Norway. Around the same time, the Soviet Union began invading other countries, such as Finland, Lithuania, Latvia, and Estonia. It also invaded Poland shortly after Germany did.

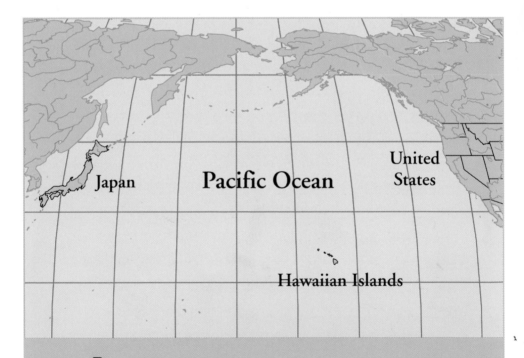

A map illustrating the distance separating Japan, Hawaii, and the United States mainland.

While war raged in Europe, conflict also arose in Asia. Since the early 1900s, Japan and Russia had fought to gain control of Manchuria, a region in northeast China. Both wanted the area's natural resources, such as coal, iron, and lead. The region also had rich soil for farming. In 1905, Japan defeated Russia in the Russo-Japanese War. By 1931, the Japanese controlled all of Manchuria.

In the 1930s, the United States grew concerned over Japan's aggressive actions. This was because America also controlled land in Asia. (U.S. territories included Wake and Midway Islands and the Philippine Islands.) In 1940, President Franklin D. Roosevelt made an important decision. He moved the heart of the U.S. Pacific Naval Fleet from California to Hawaii's Pearl Harbor, closer to Japan itself. Roosevelt believed that a strong military presence there would discourage Japan from expanding further.

By 1941, Pearl Harbor was the headquarters for the U.S. Pacific Naval Fleet. The Army, Navy, Air Force, and Marines all had bases there. The air station included four airfields: Hickam, Wheeler, Kaneohe, and Ewa. It also included Ford Island, in the middle of the harbor. On the island was a long airfield and hangars for planes. So many battleships were moored along the northeast edge of Ford Island that the area was nicknamed Battleship Row.

Japan was determined not to back down, however. In September 1940, it signed a pact with Germany and Italy that made it even more powerful. The three countries agreed that if any other country waged war against one of them, the other two would supply military and economic

*A*n infant cries amidst the rubble in Shanghai, China, after a Japanese bombing raid in 1932. In the early part of the twentieth century, Japan started aggressively attacking other countries and seizing land.

aid. Since the United States was the only major nation not involved in the war, U.S. leaders saw this agreement as an act of hostility toward America.

Shortly after the pact was formed, President Roosevelt established an embargo on oil and gasoline shipments to Japan. An embargo is when one country restricts trade with another. The United States was Japan's biggest oil and gasoline supplier. Japan badly needed those resources to run factories and operate military vehicles. The president intended to use the embargo to force Japan to make peace with the United States. Instead, Japan viewed the embargo as an act of war.[2]

As tension grew between the two countries, U.S. forces at Pearl Harbor were placed on alert. Soldiers and sailors held regular drills to be sure they were ready for war. In the fall of 1941, Secretary of State Cordell Hull met with a Japanese diplomat to try to work out a peaceful solution.

Japan, however, was already preparing for battle. Several months earlier, Admiral Isoroku Yamamoto, commander of Japan's Combined Fleet, began planning a bombing attack on Pearl Harbor. Although Yamamoto thought his country should avoid going to war with a nation as powerful as the United States, he was ready to do whatever Japan asked of him. His aim was to catch American forces by surprise. He believed Japan would have to strike first and strike hard to cripple the U.S. fleet. Then Japan would be free to keep all the territory it had seized in Asia.

Most experts who study World War II agree that Yamamoto greatly misjudged how fiercely Americans would react to a surprise attack. Many U.S. military and government officials, however, did not believe that Japan would ever attempt to start a war. They did not always pay careful attention to warnings they received.

For example, on January 27, 1941, Joseph Grew, the U.S. ambassador to Japan, heard a rumor that Japan was planning to bomb Pearl Harbor. No one is certain how the rumor began, but U.S. officials who looked into it determined that the rumor was untrue. Still, Grew was

Admiral Isoroku Yamamoto planned the Japanese attack on Pearl Harbor in 1941.

concerned. He believed that the United States would be foolish to feel a false sense of security.[3]

In July 1941, the American government cracked a secret code and read cable messages between Japanese officials. The messages said that Japan was fully prepared for war. After the oil and gasoline embargo went into effect, Japanese forces stepped up training maneuvers for a bombing raid. Near the island of Kyushu, they experimented with torpedo launches and carried out air combat exercises. Like his fellow soldiers, twenty-two-year-old bomber pilot Tatsuya Ohtawa did not know the reason for the drills, but he suspected it was extremely important. "Something is coming," he thought, as he practiced bombing runs with dummy torpedoes.[4]

In October 1941, Japanese officials secretly set a deadline of October 15 to reach a peaceful agreement with the United States. If they were unable to do so by that day, they would wage war. A newspaper article in the *Japan Times and Advertiser* a few days later proudly declared, "Japan is master of its own fate. . . . If it is necessary to fight America . . . Japan will not hesitate to defend its people and its interests. It has the power, the purpose and the plan."[5]

The Japanese fleet included sixteen destroyers, battleships, and cruisers, and three submarines. It also had six aircraft carriers carrying 189 planes. It would be extremely difficult for such a large force to sail from Japan without being detected. Instead, the vessels left one at a time over several days in mid-November 1941. They met on

November 22 in the Kuril Islands, a remote region of the Pacific north of Japan, then sailed on together. On December 2 (December 1 in Hawaii time), Vice Admiral Chuichi Nagumo, leader of the Japanese forces, received a message from Yamamoto in Japan. "Climb Mount Niitake," it read. The message, arranged ahead of time, meant "proceed with the attack as planned."[6]

Talks with the United States had failed.

T he crew aboard a Japanese carrier cheers as a fighter plane takes off for Pearl Harbor early on the morning of December 7, 1941.

CHAPTER 3

Chaos

At 6:30 A.M. on December 7, 1941, U.S. pilot William Tanner was flying about a mile out of Pearl Harbor when he spotted a submarine conning tower in the water. A conning tower is the top of a submarine. Around the same time, the destroyer U.S.S. *Ward* detected the sub and realized it was a hostile vessel. The *Ward* fired on the sub and destroyed it.[1]

At 7:00 A.M., at the Opana Mobile Radar Station on the northern tip of Oahu, Privates Joseph Lockard and George Elliott were about to go off duty. Lockard decided to leave the oscilloscope on and help Elliott practice reading it. An oscilloscope is an instrument used to display changing electrical signals. Suddenly, there was a huge "blip" on the screen—a dot that represented a group of planes flying toward the base. At first Elliott thought the oscilloscope was not working properly because the blip was so big. When Elliott alerted the Information Center at Fort Shafter, an officer told him not to worry. The flight

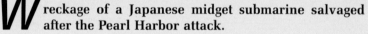

Wreckage of a Japanese midget submarine salvaged after the Pearl Harbor attack.

was probably a group of B-17 bombers due to arrive from the mainland that morning.[2]

The men did not realize that they were seeing 183 Japanese bombers and fighter planes. Commander Mitsuo Fuchida was leading them toward a massive air attack on Pearl Harbor. As the planes neared their destination, the clouds broke and Fuchida saw the U.S. Pacific Fleet laid out below him. "What a majestic sight!" he thought.[3] Moments later, he radioed the attack signal, and then a second signal—repeating three times the Japanese word for "tiger"—that meant they had achieved complete surprise. *"Tora! Tora! Tora!"* he cried.

Mary Louise Giesler was working with the U.S. Army Nurse Corps at Tripler Hospital that morning. She was helping patients onto a screened porch that overlooked the harbor. "[T]he boys were kidding around, saying, 'What is the Navy doing in bombing practice on Sunday morning?' I looked up," Giesler remembered, "and I saw those planes."[3]

The Japanese dive-bombers screamed over the Hickam, Wheeler, Kaneohe, and Ewa airfields. They

In this 1966 photo, Mitsuo Fuchida points to where he had led the Japanese planes over the mountains of Oahu on December 7, 1941. Pearl Harbor can be seen in the background.

destroyed the hangars, the barracks, and the planes arranged in rows. At Kaneohe, a soldier named Al Perucci remembered shooting open the door of a storehouse to get at the ammunition in order to fire back. It had been locked up to keep it safe from sabotage.[4]

The bombers headed for Battleship Row. Torpedoes ripped open the side of the battleship *Oklahoma*. The ship rose up, then fell back into the water and began to turn over. It sank within twenty minutes, with crew members still inside. Behind the *Oklahoma*, the *West Virginia* was hit by six torpedoes and two bombs. On the northwest side of Ford Island, dive-bombers pounded the *Raleigh* and the *Utah*. Seconds later, they hit the *Arizona* and the *Vestal*.

Billows of thick, black smoke and huge plumes of fire blanketed the area. Pearl Harbor was in chaos. Explosions, screams, machine-gun clatter, the sound of metal tearing, and the terrifying whine of attack planes filled the air. At 8:10 A.M., another bomb exploded in the *Arizona's* forecastle and detonated its forward magazines. (A forecastle is the forward part of a ship's upper deck. A magazine is a room in a ship or fort where explosive materials are stored.)

Admiral Kimmel, at home preparing for his golf game with Lieutenant General Short, received a phone call that the fleet was under attack. In his white dress uniform, he ran outside where he had a view of Battleship Row. "The sky was full of the enemy," Kimmel remembered. Just then, he saw the *Arizona* explode in a 500-foot cloud of smoke and fire. The blast lifted the 35,000-ton ship out of the water. A neighbor remembered that Kimmel's face turned "as white as the uniform he wore."[5]

The *Arizona* explosion blew crew members into the water and created a vacuum that put out the fires on the *Vestal*, moored to its port side. (A vacuum is a space where there is no air, and fire needs oxygen in the air to burn.) Commander Fuchida, who was leading the Japanese attack, was struck by the force of the explosion. "It was a hateful, mean looking red flame," he recalled, "and I knew at once that a big [gun] powder magazine had exploded."[6]

The *Arizona* sinks after an explosion in the ship's forecastle causes its forward magazines to explode.

On the morning of the Pearl Harbor attack, Admiral Kimmel was shocked when he looked up and saw a sky "full of the enemy."

More than a thousand men on the *Arizona* seemed to vanish in a flash—including the band members who had competed in the "Battle of the Bands" the night before. A few survivors escaped by swimming to the *Vestal*, but the water was in flames. It had been ignited by burning oil pouring from the damaged ships. Most of those who were not killed immediately were badly burned or lost arms or legs. All their comrades could do was get them to a hospital or to the medical ship *Solace* as quickly as possible. Many did not survive.

A "General Quarters" alarm sounded throughout the harbor, calling all sailors to battle stations. Within minutes, crewmen began returning fire at the enemy planes. Other sailors tried to help the wounded or pulled shipmates out of the water. At the airfields, planes lay in twisted ruins and hangers were in flames. When a guardhouse was hit by a bomb, the freed prisoners hurried to help defend the base. A fire brigade rushed to the airfields to put out the fires, but there was no water. The *Arizona* had sunk on top of the underground water pipes leading to Ford Island.

Soldiers grabbed any weapons they could find and fired at the planes, although it did little good. At Kaneohe, one shooter with an automatic rifle hit the fuel tank of a Japanese fighter plane. As fuel drained from the plane, the pilot turned around to fulfill orders given before the attack. He was to crash into the enemy in case of engine failure. The pilot zoomed toward the shooter, and the two men fired at one another until the plane smashed into the ground.[7]

On Battleship Row, shrapnel tore through the *West Virginia.* (Shrapnel are the metal fragments of an exploding shell.) Captain Mervyn Bennion was mortally wounded. Mess Attendant Doris Miller, a husky sailor who had competed in Pearl Harbor boxing matches, helped move Bennion to safety. He stayed with the captain until he died. Then an officer ordered Miller to man a machine gun. Miller, an African American, had never been trained for battle. In the 1940s, African-American

"above and beyond the call of duty"

DORIE MILLER
*Received the Navy Cross
at Pearl Harbor, May 27, 1942*

The image of Doris Miller was used in many Navy recruitment posters like the one above. Miller was the first African American to receive the Navy Cross.

soldiers were restricted to non-combat duty. Nevertheless, he sprang to action and joined his crewmates in defending the ship. Doris Miller became the first African American to receive the Navy Cross, one of the highest military awards for courage in battle. He would die less than two years later in the South Pacific, when a Japanese sub torpedoed the U.S.S. *Liscome Bay*.[8]

CHAPTER 4

The Second Wave

After thirty minutes, the bombing at Pearl Harbor stopped. The Japanese planes banked sharply, turned north, and flew off, leaving the harbor in flames and smoke. The attack was not over, however. After a brief pause, a second wave of 36 fighter planes and 135 bombers headed for the naval air base.

One of the most memorable moments in the attack came during the few minutes between the first and second waves. The *Nevada* had been hit hard and was listing (tilting) to port. The *Nevada* was in danger of catching fire from the flames that consumed the *Arizona* and *Tennessee*. Lieutenant Commander Francis Thomas ordered the crew of the *Nevada* to get under way. At 8:50 A.M. the ship slowly backed out of its berth. It steered around the burning ships, and headed south toward the channel leading to the sea. Three crewmen from the doomed *Arizona* scrambled aboard the *Nevada* as it passed and took positions at one of the machine guns.

The sight of the majestic but wounded battleship steaming through billows of smoke and flames was breathtaking. Hundreds of sailors watched it pass. They saw its tattered American flag raised high and its machine guns blazing, and they were inspired to fight even harder. They had no time to celebrate, however—a few minutes later, the second wave of bombing began.

A small rescue boat attempts to retrieve crewmen from the U.S.S. *West Virginia* after the ship was bombed by Japanese planes.

Now Japanese pilots aimed for ships that were undamaged. They spied the *Nevada* cruising toward the sea and swarmed around it. Their goal was to sink the ship in the narrow mouth of the harbor and block other vessels from escaping. The *Nevada* was ablaze but still returning fire when Lieutenant Commander Thomas realized what the Japanese were trying to do and ran the ship aground.[1]

At 9:30 A.M., five bombs struck Floating Dry Dock Two, where the U.S.S. *Shaw* and the tugboat *Sotoyomo* were docked. A ball of fire ignited the *Shaw*'s forward magazines. The *Shaw* exploded, shooting flames as though it were a fireworks factory. The blast was so powerful that it split the ship's bow in two.

The Pearl Harbor Naval Hospital was just south of the dry dock. Pharmacist Mate Burt Amgwert was working there, and he remembered that the horrific explosion of the *Shaw* "broke windowpanes in the hospital and blew our clothes and hair as if we were in a tornado."[2] Dr. Tully Blalock, a Medical Corps officer, also saw the fireball from across the harbor. He later helped tend wounded crew members of the *Shaw*. "Those boys were completely covered with oil, grease, soot, and smoke," he said. "All were badly burned. . . . Some had been blown overboard and swallowed a lot of oil." Dr. Blalock gave the sailors morphine, a strong pain-killer, until his supply ran out.[3]

Finally, the Japanese planes flew off for the last time. The relentless bombing had lasted only a few hours, but it left Pearl Harbor and the U.S. Pacific Fleet shattered. More than 2,400 had been killed—almost half of that number

A great ball of fire ignites the forward magazine of the U.S.S. *Shaw*. The blast was so powerful it split the ship's bow.

were from the *Arizona*. More than 1,100 Americans had been wounded. Some of the damaged ships had capsized, trapping crew members.

U.S. soldiers and sailors did manage to shoot down some of the enemy planes. Sixty-four Japanese soldiers were killed. Twenty-nine of more than 350 Japanese planes were destroyed. By Sunday afternoon, the surviving Japanese pilots had returned to their aircraft carriers. Its task completed, the Japanese fleet headed home.

CHAPTER 5

The Real McCoy

As ruinous as the attack on Pearl Harbor was, it could have been much worse. The previous year, the U.S. government had ordered Admiral Kimmel to send one-quarter of the Pearl Harbor fleet to the Atlantic Ocean. There, American forces helped Great Britain defend itself against Germany in the Battle of Britain (July–October, 1940). They escorted British supply ships and alerted allies when German vessels were in the area.

Even when it seemed certain that Japan intended to go to war with the United States, U.S. officials believed that the greatest danger was in Southeast Asia. For this reason, Admiral Kimmel was also ordered to deploy aircraft carriers to the Western Pacific Ocean. At the end of November 1941, the *Enterprise* and the *Lexington* left Pearl Harbor for Wake and Midway Islands, more than a thousand miles away. As a result of these orders, many of the ships that normally would have been in Pearl Harbor on December 7, 1941, were at sea. In addition, Japanese

Wrecked fighter planes littered Wheeler Field after the Japanese bombing of Pearl Harbor.

bombers had overlooked Pearl Harbor's fuel tank farms. These held thousands of gallons of oil that were essential for the war. The shallow waters of the harbor also allowed repairmen to refloat many of the damaged ships. These ships would have been sunk had they been at sea.

The first few hours after the attack were nearly as terrifying as the bombing itself. Parts of Honolulu were destroyed and many civilians were killed. Some of the ammunition that American soldiers used to defend against the Japanese planes was defective, and it hit streets and buildings and started fires.

At Pearl Harbor itself, the destruction was staggering. Huge ships listed or were capsized in the oily water of the harbor. Soldiers and sailors scrambled to save the injured and put out fires on ships and airfields. Rescue boats carried wounded men to Ford Island. Employees who had support jobs and were not at work during the attack later rushed to the base to help. Wherever barracks had not been destroyed, they set up temporary hospitals.

On Battleship Row, dozens of sailors were still trapped inside the *Oklahoma*, *West Virginia*, *California*, and other ships. The ship fires raged for days before burning themselves out. Rescue crews banged on hulls with wrenches or pipes and reached men trapped inside by following the tapping they heard in reply. It was Monday afternoon, December 8, almost a day and a half later by the time the last survivors on the overturned *Oklahoma* were rescued.[1]

On the *West Virginia*, sailors worked frantically to reach trapped crewmates. The fire was so fierce that the rescuers had to abandon ship on Sunday evening, even though it continued to burn. Richard Fiske, a Marine Corps musician on the *West Virginia*, remembered trying to save six men who were still trapped in the pump room two days after the attack. "We made dives to rescue them, but they were too far down," Fiske recalled. "We heard them tapping and later learned that they had lived until just before Christmas."[2]

Almost as awful as the destruction was the confusion and panic that broke out all over Oahu. In the chaos, rumors quickly spread. Some people heard that a third air

DECEMBER 7th

Remember Pearl Harbor

WORK·FIGHT·SACRIFICE

The National Cash Register Company

Wartime posters reminded Americans to "Remember Pearl Harbor."

attack was coming, or that enemy troops had landed on Honolulu's Waikiki Beach. Others heard that the drinking water had been poisoned, or that civilians of Japanese descent had aided in the attack. Some believed that the U.S. mainland was being bombed, too.

Many residents of Oahu were so used to the noise of the air base that for hours after the bombing began they did not realize an enemy attack was under way. At radio station KGMB in Honolulu, deejay Webley Edwards answered hundreds of calls from perplexed listeners. Finally, at about 9:00 A.M., he read another alert and then added, "This is the real McCoy." Many people still remember those words as the first real announcement of the bombing.[3]

That evening, Hawaii was placed under martial law. This meant that the U.S. military government took over for the Hawaiian civil government. The military set curfews to keep people off the streets at night in case of another attack. It also ordered a strict blackout—all lights off after dark. Martial law remained in effect in Hawaii until October 1944.

In the fear and dread that settled on Oahu the night of December 7, 1941, the smallest event could trigger panic. At Kaneohe airfield, a soldier touched off a 15-minute exchange of gunfire when he began shooting at a noise he heard. The gunfire set off an alarm, and when civilians drove by to see what

*P*resident Franklin Delano Roosevelt signs a declaration of war against Japan.

caused the shooting, they were also fired upon. Luckily, no one was injured.[4]

On December 8, President Roosevelt stood before Congress and delivered a forceful and angry message:

Yesterday, December 7th, 1941—a date which will live in infamy—the United States of America was suddenly and deliberately attacked by naval and air forces of the Empire of Japan. . . . Always will we remember the character of the [attack] against us. No matter how long it may take us to overcome this . . . invasion, the American people in their righteous might will win through to absolute victory. . . . I ask that the Congress declare that since the unprovoked and dastardly attack by Japan on Sunday, December 7, 1941, a state of war has existed between the United States and the Japanese Empire.

In six minutes, the president's speech was over. Congress voted to declare war within an hour.

Almost immediately, workers at Pearl Harbor began salvage and repair operations. Within two weeks, the *Pennsylvania, Maryland,* and *Tennessee* were seaworthy once more. The *Nevada,* which had proudly tried to steam out of the harbor during the attack, was ready for service again in 1942. The *Arizona* and the *Oklahoma,* however, were completely lost. At the airfields, most of the damaged planes could not be repaired, but hangars and barracks were quickly replaced.

As the United States rushed to rebuild the Pacific Fleet, angry and shocked Americans tried to understand how the country could have been caught by surprise. Ten days after the bombing, Admiral Kimmel and Lieutenant General Short were relieved of their commands. They were accused of failing to be on proper alert for an attack.

The U.S. government and military held several investigations into the Pearl Harbor disaster. In 1942, members of the first investigation, called the Roberts Commission, declared that Kimmel and Short had committed a very serious offense: dereliction of duty. This meant that they had failed to perform the duties necessary to prevent an enemy attack. Even though the two men were never formally charged with a crime, the Roberts Commission report damaged their reputations. Short left the military in February 1942 and worked for the Ford Motor Company; he died in 1949. Kimmel left the Navy in March 1942 and joined a shipbuilding firm. He died in 1968.[5]

In May 1999, the U.S. Senate and President Bill Clinton officially excused Admiral Kimmel and Lieutenant General Short from blame for the Pearl Harbor disaster. They decided that the two men had not had important information that could have warned them of an attack, such as the diplomatic messages the

*T*ourists enter the U.S.S. *Arizona* Memorial at Pearl Harbor, Hawaii, in May 2001.

government had decoded. The Senate also requested that, as a gesture of respect, the deceased men be promoted in military rank.[6]

The fury Americans felt about Pearl Harbor often boiled over into hatred directed at Japanese Americans. On February 19, 1942, President Roosevelt called Japanese Americans a "national security risk." He ordered them to report to internment camps in Arizona, Arkansas, California, Colorado, Idaho, Utah, and Wyoming. More than 110,000 people were forced to leave their homes, land, and businesses behind. They were not permitted to return until 1945.

Despite the discrimination Japanese Americans experienced, many of them bravely defended the United States in World War II. More than 1,200 Japanese Americans volunteered to join the 100th Battalion, which was stationed in Italy in 1943. Some of the same soldiers also served in another regiment whose members earned more medals than any other American unit in World War II.[7]

An important reform that resulted from the Pearl Harbor bombing was that the U.S. government reorganized to be better prepared for such disasters. In 1947, the Central Intelligence Agency (CIA) was set up to track information about foreign governments that might affect the security of the United States. In addition, Congress created the Department of Defense to bring all of the military branches under one government office.

The most deadly events of the war came four years later, although they were not a direct result of the Pearl

U.S.S. *West Virginia* veteran Richard Fiske plays a bugle at the U.S.S. *Arizona* Memorial in 1998.

Harbor disaster. On August 6 and 9, 1945, the United States dropped atomic bombs on the Japanese cities of Hiroshima and Nagasaki. The action was meant to hasten the end of World War II. The bombs killed more than 200,000 people and reduced the cities to rubble.[8] Japan surrendered on August 15, 1945.

The memory of the Pearl Harbor bombing is still vivid, even though many of the survivors have died. Tourists in Oahu can visit two sites that honor those killed that day. One is the National Memorial Cemetery of the Pacific. Almost half the Americans who died in the attack are buried there, in a volcano crater called the "Punchbowl."

The second site is the U.S.S. *Arizona* Memorial. The U.S. Navy left the battered ship where it sank, with the remains of its dead crewmen inside. A white, curved structure arches across the middle of the sunken ship. There, visitors can see the outline of the *Arizona* and its gun turret, which rises from the water. On the marble walls of a shrine room are carved the names and ranks of the crewmen who went down with the ship.

The fuel bunkers of the *Arizona* are still leaking, drop by drop. Visitors can see a faint oil slick on the water near the memorial. In 1991, a diver for the National Park Service described the droplets rising up from where he explored the wreckage. "There is a sense that the *Arizona* . . . is still bleeding slightly from one of its wounds," he observed.[9]

Only hours after the bombing ended on December 7, 1941, Radioman Lee Shannon on the U.S.S. *Argonne* recorded his thoughts about the terrible disaster. "What an unearthly, unbelievably, incredibly ghastly, gory sight and sound!" he wrote in his diary. "The complete, authentic saga of December 7 will be years in the developing. . . . Oh, there are so very many more tales."[10] More than sixty years after the Pearl Harbor attack, Shannon's words still ring true.

Other Military Disasters

PLACE	DATE	DESCRIPTION
The Boston Massacre	1770	With the Townshend Acts of 1767, Great Britain imposed duties (taxes) on various items imported to the American colonies. The colonists reacted strongly, and in 1770 a riot broke out over the issue in Boston, Massachusetts. British troops sent to maintain order and enforce the Townshend Acts killed five colonists. The Boston Massacre is considered one of the events that led to the American Revolution (1775–1783).
The Siege of the Alamo	February 24 –March 6, 1836	Mexican General Santa Anna marched several thousand soldiers into San Antonio and attempted to take the Alamo, a mission converted to a fortress that was occupied by Texas revolutionaries. For several days, 180 Texans led by Davy Crockett, William B. Travis, and James Bowie held off the Mexican troops. The Alamo's defenders were eventually wiped out, but their fierce battle inspired fighting anger among Texans. With the cry "Remember the Alamo!" Texans defeated the Mexicans six weeks later at San Jacinto.
The Battle of the Little Bighorn	June 25, 1876	Also known as "Custer's Last Stand." In early 1876, Lieutenant Colonel George Armstrong Custer's regiment joined other U.S. military troops organized to force the Sioux and Cheyenne Indians in the Montana territory onto reservations. On June 25, Custer found an Indian village in a valley along the Little Bighorn River. Custer anticipated that there would be about 1,000 warriors present. Believing his 650 soldiers could take the village, he decided to attack. In actuality, about 2,000 Indian warriors were there—possibly the largest gathering of Indian warriors in American history. In about an hour, Custer and his entire unit were killed.
The Gulf of Tonkin Resolution	August 7, 1964	On August 2, 1964, North Vietnam allegedly fired without warning on the U.S.S. Maddox in the Gulf of Tonkin. Five days later, Congress passed a resolution supporting President Lyndon B. Johnson's order to attack North Vietnamese naval bases. The Gulf of Tonkin Resolution is still controversial. It allowed the president to take "all necessary steps" to protect the forces of the United States and its allies. As a result, the United States was drawn more deeply into the Vietnamese conflict, even though a declaration of war was never made.

Chapter 1. "This Is Not A Drill!"

1. Lisa Grunwald, "The Day Before Disaster: How America Lived," *Pearl Harbor: December 7, 1941–December 7, 1991 (LIFE Collector's Edition*, Fall 1991), p. 27.

2. Gordon W. Prange, *At Dawn We Slept: The Untold Story of Pearl Harbor* (New York: Penguin Books, 1991), p. 411.

3. Thomas Mathews, et al., "Remembering Pearl Harbor," *Newsweek*, November 25, 1991, p. 38.

4. Otto Friedrich, "Day of Infamy," *Time*, December 2, 1991, p. 30.

5. Prange, *At Dawn We Slept*, p. 517.

6. Mathews, "Remembering Pearl Harbor," p. 35.

Chapter 2. "The Power, the Purpose, and the Plan"

1. Hawaii Department of Business, Economic Development, and Tourism (DBEDT), "Table 1.01—Population of Counties: 1831 To 1990," *DBEDT Census Page*, January 1, 1997, <http://www.hawaii.gov/dbedt/2000/010197.html> (March 9, 2001).

2. Gordon W. Prange, *At Dawn We Slept: The Untold Story of Pearl Harbor* (New York: Penguin Books, 1991), pp. 167–171.

3. Ibid., p. 31.

4. Thomas Mathews, et al., "Remembering Pearl Harbor," *Newsweek*, November 25, 1991, p. 33.

5. Prange, *At Dawn We Slept*, p. 279.

6. Edwin P. Hoyt, *Japan's War* (New York: Da Capo Press, 1989), p. 220.

Chapter 3. Chaos

1. Thomas Mathews, et al., "Remembering Pearl Harbor," *Newsweek*, November 25, 1991, p. 35.

2. Ibid.

3. Susan Bolotin, ed., *Pearl Harbor: December 7, 1941–December 7, 1991 (LIFE*, Fall 1991), p. 36.

4. Ibid., p. 38.

5. Otto Friedrich, "Day of Infamy," *Time*, December 2, 1991, p. 44.

6. Terence McComas, *Pearl Harbor: Fact and Reference Book—Everything To Know About December 7, 1941* (Honolulu, Hawaii: Mutual Publishing, 1991), p. 112.

7. Friedrich, "Day of Infamy," p. 44.

8. Department of the Navy, Naval Historical Center, "Ship's Cook Third Class Doris Miller, USN." *Naval Historical Center*, March 29, 1999, <http://www.history.navy.mil/faqs/faq57-4.htm> (February 28, 2001).

Chapter 4. The Second Wave

1. Donald M. Goldstein, Katherine V. Dillon, and J. Michael Wenger, *The Way It Was: Pearl Harbor—The Original Photographs* (Dulles, Va.: Brassey, Inc., 1995), pp. 98–105.

2. Otto Friedrich, "Day of Infamy," *Time*, December 2, 1991, p. 34.

3. Thomas Mathews, et al., "Remembering Pearl Harbor," *Newsweek*, November 25, 1991, p. 37.

Chapter 5. The Real McCoy

1. Otto Friedrich, "Day of Infamy," *Time*, December 2, 1991, p. 45.

2. Susan Bolotin, ed., *Pearl Harbor: December 7, 1941–December 7, 1991* (*LIFE*, Fall 1991), p. 45.

3. Terence McComas, *Pearl Harbor: Fact and Reference Book—Everything To Know About December 7, 1941* (Honolulu, Hawaii: Mutual Publishing, 1991), p. 114.

4. Gordon W. Prange, *At Dawn We Slept: The Untold Story of Pearl Harbor* (New York: Penguin Books, 1991), p. 569.

5. McComas, pp. 100–103.

6. Jonathan S. Landay, "Officers Join Effort to Exonerate Pearl Harbor Commanders," *Philadelphia Inquirer*, November 24, 1999, p. A4.

7. McComas, p. 104.

8. "Thousands Pause to Remember When Hiroshima Became 'Hell on Earth.'" CNN.com Asianow East, August 6, 2000, <http://www.cnn.com/2000/ASIANOW/east/08/06/hiroshima.anniversary/index.html> (February 28, 2001).

9. Daniel J. Lenihan, "The Arizona Revisited: Divers Explore the Legacy of Pearl Harbor," Natural History, November 1991, National Park Service Government Submerged Cultural Resources Unit, October 15, 1998, <http://www.nps.gov/scru/revisit2.html> (March 2, 2001).

10. Susan Bolotin, ed., Pearl Harbor: December 7, 1941–December 7, 1991 (*LIFE*, Fall 1991), p. 35.

aggressive—Showing readiness to attack.

airfield—The landing field of an airport.

ambassador—A person sent as the chief government representative to another country.

berth—A place where a ship lies at anchor or at a wharf.

bow—The forward part of a ship.

civilian—A person not enrolled in the military.

conning tower—A raised structure on the deck of a submarine used to navigate and to direct attacks.

cruiser—A large, fast warship, but smaller than a battleship.

curfew—An order or law requiring certain or all people to be off the streets at a stated time.

deploy—To spread out or place in position for some purpose.

destroyer—A small, fast warship armed with guns, depth charges, torpedoes, and sometimes guided missiles.

diplomat—A person who helps arrange agreements or conducts talks between nations.

discrimination—Treating some people differently without any fair or proper reason.

dive-bomber—An airplane designed for dropping bombs.

dry dock—A landing that is kept dry for repairing or building ships.

economic—Relating to the production, distribution, and consumption of goods and services.

embargo—The restriction of trade imposed by one country upon another.

forecastle—The forward part of the upper deck of a ship.

gun turret—A low, usually rotating structure on a tank, warship, or airplane in which guns are mounted.

hangar—A shed or other closed shelter for housing and repairing aircraft.

hostility—An unfriendly or enemy attitude or action.

infamy—An evil reputation brought about by criminal, shocking, or brutal behavior.

internment—The state of being confined, especially during a war.

list (verb)—To lean to one side or tilt, as a ship.

magazine—A room in a fort or ship in which gun powder and other explosives are kept.

maneuver—An exercise by armed forces.

moor—To fasten in place with cables, lines, or anchors.

oscilloscope—An instrument that displays variations in electrical quantity as waves on a screen or monitor.

port—Looking forward, the left side of a ship or aircraft.

sabotage—A destructive or blocking action by enemy agents or sympathizers to make a nation's war effort more difficult.

salvage—The act of saving a ship or possessions in danger of being lost.

shrapnel—Metal pieces from an exploded bomb, shell, or mine.

starboard—Looking forward, the right side of a ship or aircraft.

torpedo—A cylindrical self-propelled underwater weapon.

vacuum—A space from which air has been removed.

Allen, Thomas B. *Remember Pearl Harbor: American and Japanese Survivors Tell Their Story.* Washington D.C.: National Geographic Society, 2001.

Anthony, Nathan, and Robert Gardner. *The Bombing of Pearl Harbor in American History.* Berkeley Heights, N.J.: Enslow Publishers, Inc., 2001.

Goldstein, Donald M., Katherine V. Dillon, and J. Michael Wenger. *The Way It Was: Pearl Harbor—The Original Photographs.* Dulles, Va.: Brassey, Inc., 1995.

Hasday, Judy L. *Pearl Harbor.* Broomall, Pa.: Chelsea House Publishers, 2000.

Sullivan, George E. *The Day Pearl Harbor Was Bombed: A Photo History of World War II.* New York: Scholastic, Inc., 1991.

Tanaka, Shelley. *Attack on Pearl Harbor: The True Story of the Day America Entered World War II.* New York: Hyperion Books for Children, 2001.

Taylor, Theodore. *Air Raid—Pearl Harbor!: The Story of December 7, 1941.* New York: Harcourt Children's Books, 2001.

Wels, Susan. *Pearl Harbor: America's Darkest Day: December 7, 1941.* Alexandria, Va.: Time-Life Custom Publishing, 2001.

Internet Addresses

EyeWitness: Attack at Pearl Harbor, 1941
http://www.ibiscom.com/pearl.htm

Hawaii Guide: History of Pearl Harbor
http://www.hawaiiguide.com/history.htm

Surfing the Net with Kids: Pearl Harbor
http://www.surfnetkids.com/pearlharbor.htm